Basic
Book Repair
Methods

Basic
Book Repair
Methods

Abraham A. Schechter
Simmons College
Graduate School of Library & Information Science
Boston

Illustrated by the Author

1999

LIBRARIES
U N L I M I T E D
A Member of the Greenwood Publishing Group

Westport, Connecticut • London

Libraries Unlimited
A member of Greenwood Publishing Group, Inc.
88 Post Road West,
Westport, CT 06881
www.lu.com

Library of Congress Cataloging-in-Publication Data

Schechter, Abraham A.
    Basic book repair methods / Abraham A. Schechter ; illustrated by the author.
       ix, 102 p.   22x28 cm.
    Includes bibliographical references and index.
    ISBN 1-56308-700-6 (pbk.)
    1. Books--Conservation and restoration.   I. Title.
Z701.S34   1999
025.8'4--dc21
                                                                98-50950
                                                                    CIP

P

In order to keep this title in print and available to the academic community, this edition was produced using digital reprint technology in a relatively short print run. This would not have been attainable using traditional methods. Although the cover has been changed from its original appearance, the text remains the same and all materials and methods used still conform to the highest book-making standards.

Contents

Preface

Welcome. *Basic Book Repair Methods* addresses some common preservation techniques that invariably become necessary in library and archival collections of any size. From the cleaning of pages and their readhesion, to case reattachment and rebacking, the solutions provided here are geared primarily to general, non-valuable materials. These types of books and documents represent the kinds most popularly needed and circulated by readers and researchers.

The recommended repair methods can be accomplished using tools and supplies that are both easily obtained and useful for multiple purposes. The procedures are described in chronological sequence, and photographs show the techniques from the viewpoint of the operator—the person actually doing the work. This manual may be used by anyone interested in the repair and maintenance of books (professional and nonprofessional alike) and *Basic Book Repair Methods* can serve as a teaching tool for workshop groups and materials repair departments. Users of this manual will see how the repair procedures are at once uncomplicated and produce remarkable results. I recommend some practice with expendable, non-collection materials for the refinement of these valuable skills.

Preserving print materials is integral to any collection's mission, large or small. By maintaining complete, usable source materials, the information stays available to users. By accomplishing repair work in-house, the materials can be treated promptly and kept available. Two other valuable attributes in setting up an in-house repair area concern its cost-effectiveness and the ability to choose supplies and procedures of the highest quality and permanence. This book provides a starting point with respect to methodology, good craft habits, and tools. I wish readers much success and enjoyment in their work.

Acknowledgments

I would like to express my thanks to the faculty and students of Simmons College Graduate School of Library and Information Science, particularly Dr. Sheila S. Intner and Professors A. J. Anderson and Megan Sniffin-Marinoff. A great thanks to Mr. Todd Pattison of the Northeast Document Conservation Center. I am also deeply grateful to my parents, Irene and David Schechter, for their unceasing support.

Thanks, Mom and Dad!

1
Cleaning Paper

About the Cleaning of Paper

Paper-based materials designated for cleaning will have been noted, either through user circulation or a collection survey, that there are handling marks and stains which require repair. Specifically for a basic repair unit, we are referring to dry-cleaning treatments, as opposed to bleaching, washing, and deacidification treatments practiced in specialized conservation laboratories. Dry-cleaning paper and erasing marks should be accomplished at a well-lit work table and in a short time, using simple, non-hazardous tools. Clean, well-maintained library and archival materials are respectful to both user and text alike and extend the collections' usable and stable life.

Dry-cleaning procedures are appropriately applied on paper with handwritten marks and surface debris. This is to say marks that have been put on the paper by handling, through both repeated and careless use, as opposed to paper discoloration owing to acidic papers and glues. All the tools involved in dry cleaning are friction devices, in varying degrees, from the soft drafting brush to the coarser erasure particles.

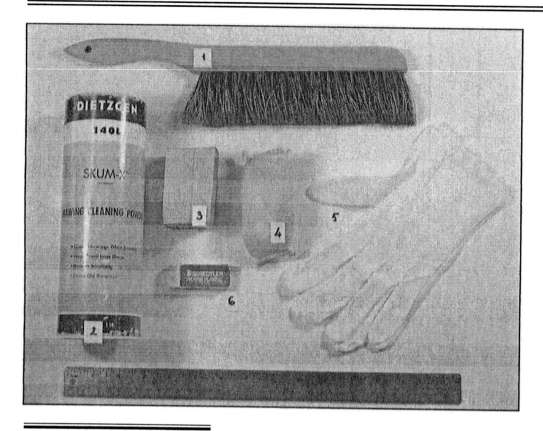

Figure 1—Cleaning tools: (1) drafting brush, (2) Skum-X® cleaning powder, (3) Smoke-off sponge, (4) cleaning pad, (5) cotton gloves, (6) white plastic eraser.

Sequence for Using Cleaning Tools

Brushing: On a clean, level work surface, holding the material to be cleaned carefully and securely, lightly brush in a direction that is away from where you are situated. You will be loosening and removing superficial surface particles from the paper. In a bound volume, brush away from the book's "gutter" so that particles do not collect where the pages are joined. The book or document may be turned to accommodate more convenient cleaning. You may choose to work on top of a sheet of paper, as the particulates will offset from the cleaned material onto the work surface.

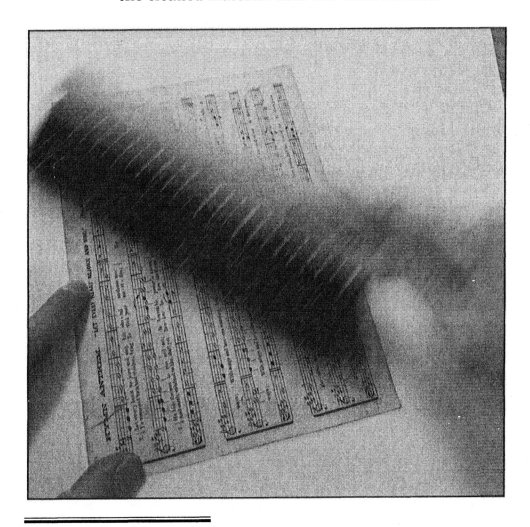

Figure 2—Brushing technique.

Smoke-off Sponge: After the paper has been superficially cleaned by brushing, with a careful, secure hold, wipe the paper with a smoke-off sponge, working from the center to the edges. Work in sweeping strokes, from one direction, remembering that with increased friction comes the possibility of damaging the paper's fragile surface, or accidently removing a page from a volume. Additional surface debris will be absorbed by the smoke-off sponge. As the sponge darkens, trim it with scissors to expose a clean working surface.

Eraser: In a motion similar to that used for the smoke-off sponge, use a white plastic (Staedtler® or comparable type) eraser, working in one direction. Erasers are most effective for cleaning smaller areas. With an abrasion that is stronger than the smoke-off sponge, handwritten marks and more stubborn stains can be removed. When bearing down on the material, work deliberately, and note the easy possibility of crumpling the paper.

Cleaning Pad: Cleaning pads (also referred to as "opaline" pads) hold fine erasing particles within a porous cloth enclosure. For areas that cannot be effectively cleaned by brushing and light erasing, this type of granular erasing material can be used. The pad itself is not actually used on the paper, but instead is used as a dispenser of the particles by shaking the pad above the surface stain. The erasing particles are then worked into the stain, in a light, circular motion. The heel of a bare hand is suggested, as pressure can be controlled and abrasion kept to a minimum. As the erasing particles collect debris, they will darken. Closely watch the area being cleaned, aware always that abrasives which are stronger than soft erasers can remove ink as well as stains and debris.

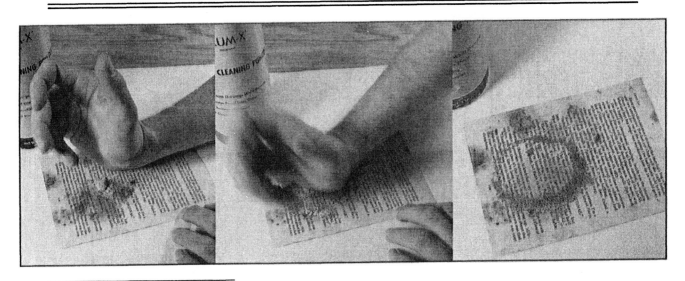

Figure 3—Before, during, and after removing a stain using granular erasing powder.

Cleaning Powder: A more coarse granular erasing tool than cleaning pads is Skum-X® cleaning powder. This can be applied when the finer grain dispensed from a pad cannot sufficiently remove foreign matter. In the same application as with cleaning pads, Skum-X® is sprinkled directly onto the area to be treated, then carefully worked into that area, using a circular motion. As with all the previous procedures, frequently interrupt your work to survey the detectable changes to the paper material. An area can be "over-cleaned"; images and text can be removed along with the unwanted marks. By consistently surveying your work, you will arrive at the balance between a cleaned surface and bold, saturated print.

Postscriptum

Paper cleaning is accompanied by a selection process. Not only must the appropriate tools be chosen, but the materials to be cleaned, and to what extent cleaning is required, must be determined. Dry-cleaning each single page in a volume must be determined with consultation and consideration. If extensive cleaning in one bound volume is called for, try to use a method that creates a minimum of erasure debris that can threaten to lodge in the binding. Prioritization for thorough cleaning will be most important in the cases of extreme staining and debris, the effects of mold, and for the purposes of exhibition presentation.

2
Mending Paper

About the Mending of Paper

Paper mending, in a basic repair unit, includes some simple and convenient treatments to prevent cuts and tears found in documents and books from aggrandizing into permanent loss.

The more archival and library materials are handled, as it can be seen in the need to clean paper, the more vulnerable they are to damage. With the staff's careful survey, materials to be mended can be selected, along with the type of mending treatment to apply. This book examines the tools and their procedures, and when they are most applicable—from the simplest pressure-sensitive adhesive to repairs involving two types of repair tissue. As with any repair procedure, work should not begin without a clean, level, and well-lit work table. A surface covering of blotting paper or a piece of mat board is recommended.

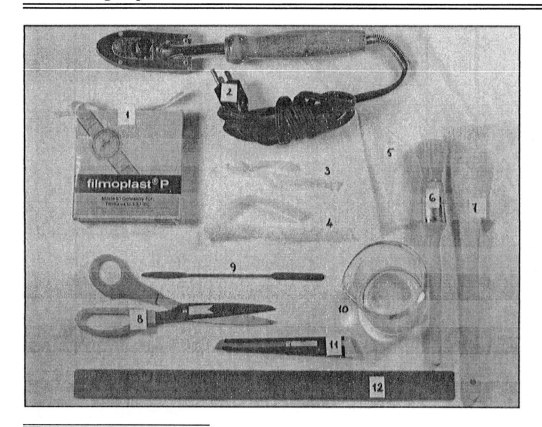

Figure 4—Mending tools: (1) pressure-sensitive tape, (2) tacking iron, (3) heat-set tissue, (4) Japanese repair paper, (5) Reemay® polyester release tissue, (6) and (7) various brushes for applying adhesives, (8) scissors, (9) microspatula, (10) wheat-starch paste, (11) Olfa® knife, (12) ruler.

Mending with Pressure-Sensitive Tape

Required Materials:

- A lightweight, stable-adhesive, acid-free tape, such as document repair tape or Filmoplast®-P transparent tape.

- Scissors.

This procedure has the advantage of convenience of use and minimal equipment requirements. Tape is particularly useful for "clean cuts," which may have been made by scissors or mat knives. Be advised, however, that tape should not be applied to fragile and rare materials. Repair tissues (including Japanese paper) will be more appropriate for brittle and antique books and documents. On the other hand, acid-free repair tape is a far superior alternative for the common paper tears, which may have been previously subjected to household/office adhesive tapes.

Figure 5—Applying pressure-sensitive tape to a paper tear.

Procedure: Pressure-sensitive tapes are usually packaged in dispenser boxes. Simply extract an appropriate length of tape, and cut the tape to accommodate the tear in the paper. Flatten the torn (or cut) area, so that the smallest comfortable seam is visible. Lower the cut section of tape carefully over the seam without stretching the tape, but simply lowering it down. This kind of tape is much thinner than household tape, and it crinkles easily. Once lowered into place, the tape can be gently hand-burnished to the paper.

Mending with Heat-Set Tissue

Required Materials:

- Tacking iron, such as the type produced by Seal®, widely used in photographic dry-mounting.

- Heat-set tissue, made with neutral pH tissue combined with an acrylic adhesive, such as that produced by the Library of Congress, or Filmoplast®-R Heat Set. Filmoplast®-R is sold both in sheets and ¾-inch dispensable rolls.

- Reemay® polyester release tissue.

Procedure: This dry process is particularly conducive for brittle papers, including brittle nineteenth-century manufactured papers. Heat-set tissue also works well on newsprint paper.

1. **Pre-heat the tacking iron.**

   The adhesive in the tissue is activated by heat, so begin by setting the tacking iron to a temperature no greater than 250°F (120°C). While making sure the tacking iron is cradled on a heat-resistant surface, allow approximately 10 minutes for the temperature to stabilize.

2. **Prepare the cleaned, torn area for treatment.**

   Gently situate the broken area so that a minimal seam is visible. If an overlap of paper fibers is visible when the two edges are placed together, reposition the edges so that they match the direction of the tear.

Figure 6—Heat-set tissue trimmed to the size of the paper tear.

3. **Superficially tack the cut piece of tissue over the tear**.

After cutting a piece of heat-set tissue to accommodate the size of the tear, place the tissue section—shiny side down (this is the acrylic adhesive side)—over the tear seam. At this point, very lightly tap the tissue down to the paper with the tacking iron; this is simply to position the tissue upon the paper.

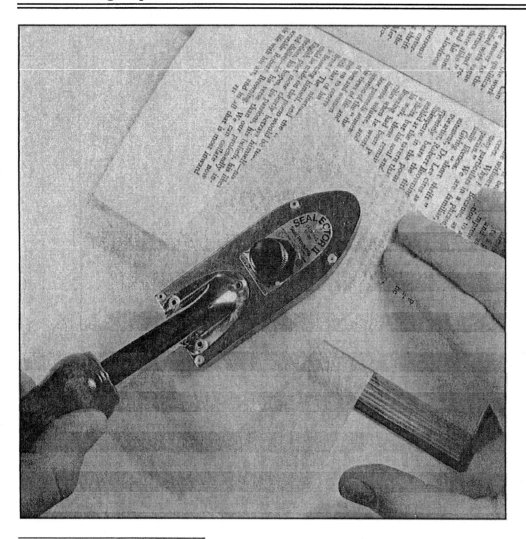

Figure 7—Heat pressing with tacking iron and Reemay®.

4. **Cover both sides of paper with Reemay® and heat press**.
    With Reemay® release tissue above and below the treated area, carefully press with the flat surface of the tacking iron. Hold down steadily for 10 seconds. Allow paper to cool, then peel back the top layer of Reemay® and examine the torn area to confirm the repair. Reemay® will not adhere to the paper. If the heat-set tissue is not completely adhered, re-iron the area after replacing the top layer of Reemay®, then re-examine.

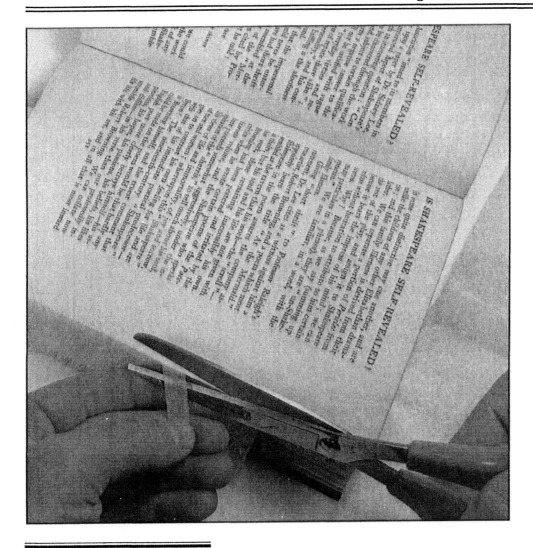

Figure 8—Trimming excess tissue to size against the paper's edge.

Postscriptum

For longer tears and heavier paper stocks, treatment with heat-set tissue is recommended for both sides of the paper. By treating both sides, the repair will resist a "tenting" effect, which, through ordinary handling, can lead to further paper damage and a re-tearing of the same area. If the area to be repaired runs out to the edge of the paper (as opposed to a cut in the center), allow for some excess tissue length, which can be trimmed off after heat setting (see Figure 8) with either scissors or an Olfa® knife.

Mending with Wheat-Starch Paste and Japanese Paper

Required Materials:

- Japanese paper: Used for repair, such as Kozo paper. This type of paper is tissue-thin, yet long-fibered and strong. Tear sheets of this type of paper into usable strips by drawing intermittent lines with a narrow paintbrush moistened with water along the direction of the grain, then separating the paper into strips.

- Wheat-starch paste: Made by cooking wheat starch in distilled water. This adhesive will blend into and strengthen the paper as well as provide the adhesive for the Japanese paper. (See Appendix 1 for a recipe for wheat-starch paste.)

- Paint brush: For the application of the wheat-starch paste onto the repair paper.

- Microspatula: To assist in the specific placement of the paste-moistened repair paper.

- Reemay®: Polyester release tissue.

- Tacking iron: Maintained at a lower temperature than for heat-setting tissue, to be used as a drying instrument after the repair paper is in place.

Procedure: This repair process is the time-honored preference of paper conservators. The Japanese handmade repair papers are flexible and strong. The wheat-starch paste is a strong, non-deteriorating adhesive that blends into the paper fibers and dries clear. This process is recommended for repairing other handmade papers, as well as sturdy older papers. The process involves a water-based adhesive, and that must be accompanied by an awareness of the response of paper to moisture. You will want to apply enough adhesive to fasten the repair paper to the torn area, but not an excess to cause the material to buckle. A warm tacking iron is useful for drying the treated area.

1. **Prepare torn material for treatment.**

   As with all mending processes, the work table should be clean and covered. The tear (or break in the paper) should be aligned and flat, with the minimum comfortable seam between the edges. Set the paper on top of a layer of Reemay®, and in the case of a bound volume, place a sheet of Reemay® underneath the page to be treated.

2. **Adhere Japanese repair paper to torn material.**

   Lightly coat a strip of Japanese paper with the wheat-starch adhesive, as opposed to brushing adhesive onto the material to be repaired. Doing the latter will certainly cause an excess of unnecessary moisture. Coating the repair paper may be done with a clean paintbrush (that has not been used on any dyed liquids or acids) using a sparing amount of wheat-starch paste. You may also use a finger as an applicator. When wet, the repair paper becomes extremely delicate.

   Carefully lower the adhesive-coated repair paper onto the tear. For more delicate placement and to maintain the flatness of the wet repair paper, the microspatula will be a useful tool.

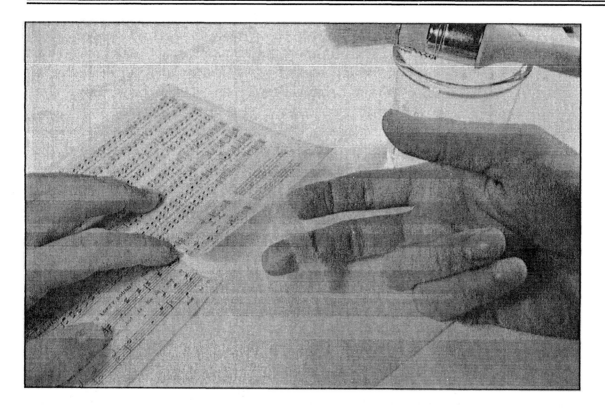

Figure 9—Japanese repair paper is both strong-fibered and translucent.

3. **Fasten repair paper securely to the material**.

Gently tap the wet repair tissue, so that it is placed flat on the seam of the mended area. After this, cover the treated area with a dry layer of Reemay® and compress more firmly. Keep the Reemay® in place and apply the warm tacking iron to dry the area. Allowing the treated area to air-dry increases the possibility of the material buckle-drying; that is to say, the material would dry with a wavy contour and would require a book press for re-flattening.

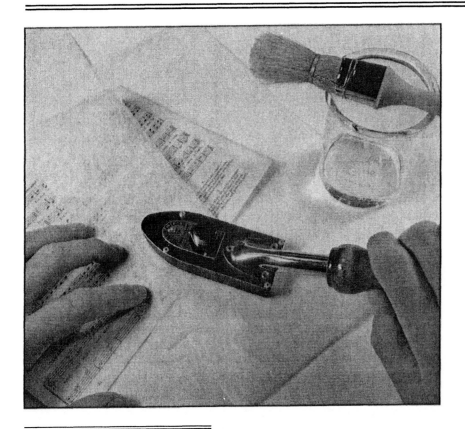

Figure 10—Heat-drying the repair. Note the Reemay® tissue surrounding the treated area.

Postscriptum

Similarly to the heat-set mending process, if the break or tear runs out to the edge of a sheet of paper, it is best to use a strip of repair paper that is longer than needed, and then trim the excess after the repair dries. Repairing both sides will not be necessary, as "tenting" is more likely with heat-set tissue. An exception would be if a heavy paper stock was being repaired. The question may arise concerning the opacity of repair papers; a lightweight Japanese paper is recommended for use so that the readability of the print remains unimpaired after the repair.

Mending Tears by Directly Applying Wheat-Starch Paste

In the case of the type of tear generally caused by careless page-turning, creating a break that reveals a wedge of paper fibers beneath the surface, a repair may be made by applying wheat-starch paste directly to the interlocking edges of the tear. Use a microspatula for this type of adhesive application. The follow-through would be the same as with repair paper, using Reemay® and a tacking iron to spot-dry. Not all tears are conducive to this type of repair, as most torn edges are clean cuts, not exposing enough fibers.

With multiple options available for paper repair, one must determine which is most appropriate. These decisions are best made not only through consultation with management at the institution, but also with consideration for the material itself. Is the material part of a circulating collection, or is it part of a historical collection that does not leave the reading room? There are physical aspects to consider, such as the type of paper and extent of damage. Often, adhesive tape is quickly applied, sending "sidelined" materials back onto the circulating field faster. The ease of use of a repair process will be a factor when choices are considered. Between heat-set and Japanese repair paper applied with wheat-starch paste, results are similar. However, heat-set is easier to use, but Japanese repair paper provides paper reinforcement and has an effective track record over a long period of time.

3
Book Hinge Tightening

Textblock and Case

Figure 11—Textblock and case components; (1) super, (2) case,
(3) textblock, (4) endpapers—which, with the super, attach
the textblock to the case.

About Book Hinge Tightening

When we refer to hinge tightening, we are addressing the problem caused by the "de-lamination," or loosening, of the textblock from the case (the hardcover). Loosening hinges are generally results of excessive handling. Heavy textblocks "drop" even as the books stand upright on the shelves, and certainly a fall down the chute of a library book-drop compounds the problem of weakened hinges. Apart from physical handling, particularly with older books, simply the age of an original adhesive can lead to fragile hinges. These are all factors to bear in mind while processing circulating materials. Once a book is flagged, hinge tightening is a simple and fast repair. If left unattended, the textblock will inevitably loosen and break from the book's case.

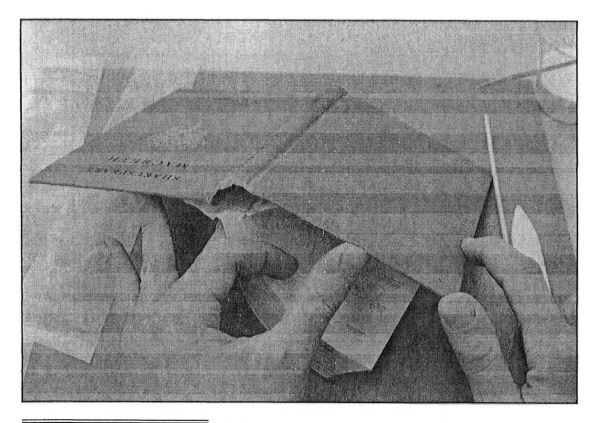

Figure 12—Textblock has "dropped" from the case; the hinges require tightening.

Required Materials:

- Wooden skewers to be used as adhesive applicators and as ridge-burnishing supports. This is the type which can be purchased in inexpensive quantity at supermarkets.

- PVA adhesive. This is Polyvinyl Acetate glue, which is manufactured to archival standards. PVA is a neutral-pH adhesive; it is white but dries clear and is non-yellowing, flexible after drying, and water-soluble.

- Brush. Make sure the brush is clean and has not been used for purposes involving dyes or acidic solutions.

- Bone folding tool. Will be used as a burnishing tool.

- Waxed paper. Will be used as an interleaving material, acting as a non-sticking barrier between the textblock and the case. Any household type is fine.

- Paper towels or clean rags. To clean off excess PVA from materials and hands. (PVA is not dangerous to handle.) Keep some on hand for all adhesive-based processes.

Procedure: Remember that the reattachment of a loose textblock by hinge tightening is appropriate when the textblock is still attached to the case. In this particular process, no new materials are being added to the book.

1. **Brush PVA adhesive onto a skewer.**

    Hold one tip of a clean skewer and rotate it, while brushing on PVA adhesive. Use care not to excessively coat the skewer; simply "cover" it with PVA.

2. **Apply adhesive.**

    Carefully hold de-laminated area open, and apply adhesive by rolling the PVA-covered skewer on the "underside" of the endpaper. The PVA will offset precisely onto the inside of the endpaper and the exposed part of the super. Make sure not to allow any adhesive to affect the spine of the book, thus endangering the case's flexibility.

3. **Close the book.**

    With waxed paper interleaving between the inside of the case and the textblock, and at the top and bottom of the textblock, close the book flat on the work surface. The waxed paper protects the pages from the effects of excess PVA escaping from the hinges during burnishing.

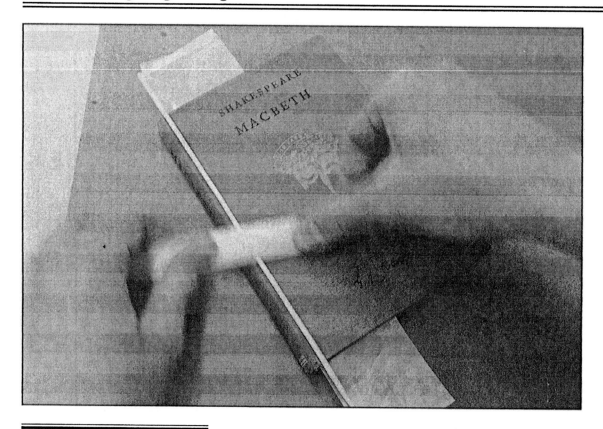

Figure 13—Burnishing with bone folding tool, skewer (situated in the exterior joint), and waxed paper interleaving.

4. **Burnish the hinge.**

Set a clean, dry skewer in the exterior joint (the outer ridge of the case) and burnish with the flat portion of the bone folding tool. Make sure the work surface is stable as you will be applying some pressure and running the bone folder along the skewer set in the exterior joint. Use care not to scratch the case in the process.

5. **Allow to dry.**

At this point, any excess adhesive should be wiped off the book. With the waxed paper interleaving still inside the case, leave the book flat to dry. The adhesive should solidify in approximately 15 minutes.

Figure 14—Completed repair.

Postscriptum

If the book to be repaired has a dust jacket, remember to remove it before starting the process. In this process, be careful not to allow adhesive to glue the spine to the case. For this reason, and to limit the necessity of cleaning excess adhesive, use a single, thin coating of PVA on the skewer. For this repair PVA is preferable over wheat-starch paste, as it is both strong and flexible once dry. PVA is also thicker and more concentrated than wheat-starch paste.

4
Repairing Interior Hinges

About Repairing Interior Hinges

A broken, or split, interior hinge refers to a break in the endpaper—specifically at the fold. An interior hinge, broken at the "gutter," exposes the super (the gauze material attached to both the spine and the endpaper). The following repair process would apply if the book's textblock is still tight to the case, with the endpaper still intact except for the split hinge.

Required Materials:

- Adhesive. Wheat-starch paste <u>or</u> PVA adhesive; both are fine for this process.

- Brush. For application of adhesive. Be sure it is clean and un-contaminated by dyes or acidic residues.

- Japanese repair paper. Cut into strips to accommodate the area to be treated. The length should match that of the book's interior hinge; allow for some excess breadth (overlapping the split hinge) for reinforcement.

- Waxed paper. Upon which to brush swatches of adhesive.

- Microspatula. To specify the placement of adhesive-saturated repair paper, and to prevent its breaking during handling.

Procedure: With repair materials at the ready, place the long side of the hinge parallel to the near edge of your work table (see Figure 15). This process centers around the lowering of an adhesive-backed strip of Japanese repair paper onto a split hinge, then carefully shaping the repair paper into place with a microspatula.

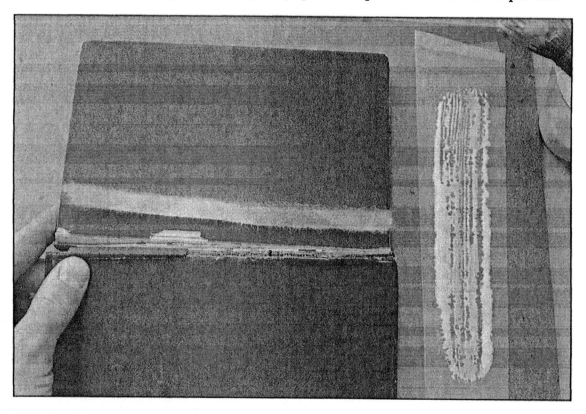

Figure 15—A split interior hinge with Japanese repair paper and a swatch of PVA brushed on waxed paper.

1. **Cut repair paper to size.**

   With an appropriately sized width of Japanese repair paper, cut the strip to conform with the length of the book's hinge. A heavier weight of repair paper may be used than the type employed in the repair of pages. The same type of weight may also be used, provided that the bulkiness of both case and textblock are not significant. With heavier books, layers of thinner repair paper work very well on split hinges.

2. **Apply adhesive to split hinge.**

   Begin by applying adhesive sparingly with the sharp end of a brush directly to the split in the book's hinge. If the super is intact, there should not be the possibility of adhesive interfering with the spine.

3. **Coat waxed paper with adhesive.**

   On a strip of waxed paper, paint a swatch of adhesive that exceeds the length of your cut strip of repair paper. Place the repair paper on the swatch.

4. **Placement of the repair paper strip.**

   Pry up the repair paper from the adhesive swatch with the microspatula. Use care not to contort the corners or edges of the repair paper. No cause for hurry here because the repair paper will not adhere to the waxed paper. Carefully lower the adhesive-backed repair paper strip to the split hinge. Lower the strip without stretching or breaking it, making sure that one end of the strip will not be hanging over one of the book's edges.

5. **Situating the repair paper strip.**

   Remember that a degree of flexibility is necessary for the opening and closing of books. Bearing this in mind, carefully "mold" the applied repair paper into place with both microspatula and fingers. Straighten out any wrinkles in the repair paper. If desired, another layer of repair paper may be added to the first one.

6. **Allow repair to dry.**

   The repair work will solidify fastest if the book is left open to air-dry. Completion can be confirmed by touching the hinge.

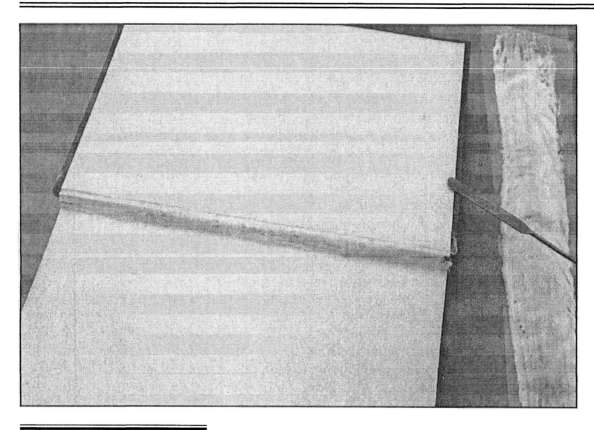

Figure 16—Completed work—book is left open to air-dry.

Postscriptum

Remember to "mold" the adhered repair paper over the split hinge for purposes of the book's flexibility—with practice—neither too loosely nor too tightly. For stability, particularly as the book is drying, create a level area for the case by propping up the non-textblock cover with another book (or any comparable-height hard surface) underneath. For endpapers of various colors, some toned repair papers are also available.

5
Hinging-In Pages

About Hinging-In Pages

Hinging-in becomes necessary when pages have come detached, either by tearing or breaking off from an otherwise intact textblock. In this repair process, a specifically sized hinge is made and adhered to the loose page. The hinged page is then adhered to the textblock. As opposed to the tipping-in of pages, hinging-in provides for more secure, full movement of a reattached page. Tipping-in simply attaches one page directly to another, limiting the overall flexibility of the paper involved in the treatment. If a book's missing pages cannot be located (and it is deemed worthy of restoration) an identical edition may be retrieved (perhaps through interlibrary loan) and the needed pages photocopied onto archival paper, and hinged into the incomplete book.

Double-sided copying is suggested, should this event arise, minimizing bulk in the textblock. If a significant section of a torn page has been lost, narrowing the page, a wider strip of heavier Japanese paper should be used to act as both filler and hinge.

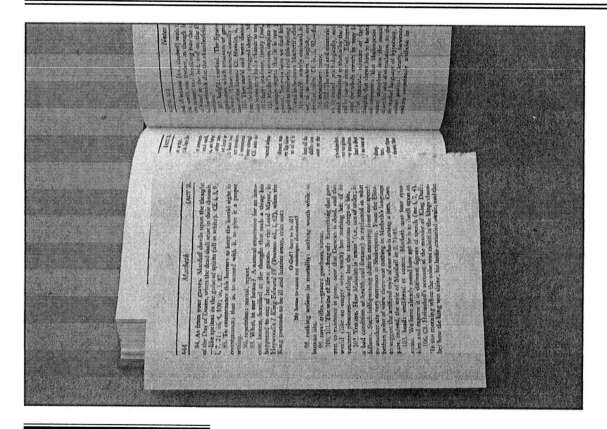

Figure 17—A page torn from a book.

Required Materials:

- Wheat-starch paste, which is a thin, workable adhesive. PVA may be used as a second choice, as the hinged page may be less workable (movable) during adhesion. Excess wheat-starch paste (in case any extends beyond the hinge, in toward the rest of the page) will dry into the paper without showing a trace.

- Brush. As always, clean and free of contaminants.

- Scrap paper. Clean sheets of paper larger than the pages to be worked on.

- Japanese repair paper to be used as hinges.

- Olfa® knife in case trimming is needed, when finishing the repair work.

- Metal ruler or one with a metal edge.

- Cardboard or matboard scraps to be used as cutting surfaces.

- Scissors for trimming hinges before adhering pages into books.

Procedure: Make sure your work surface is covered as you will be brushing paste at two points in the repair. Good lighting is also particularly emphasized here; setting in the page must be done with careful precision.

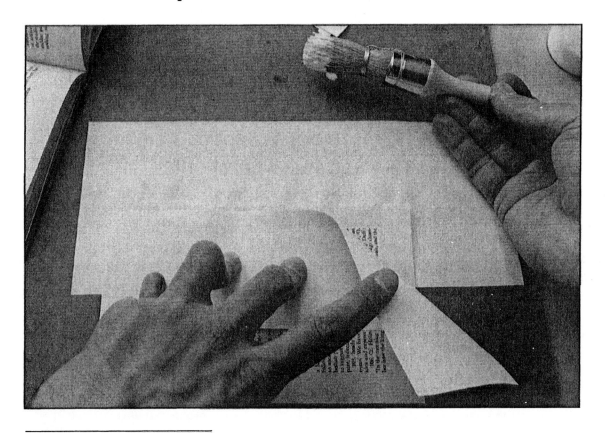

Figure 18—Application of hinge to page with adhesive, using masking technique.

1. **Adhere hinge to paper edge.**

   Begin by cutting a strip of Japanese repair paper (approximately ¾" wide) to accommodate the length of the page to be hinged. The repair paper strip will become the hinge. Now to properly adhere the hinge to the page apply adhesive with a *masking* method. Figure 18 shows a broken part of the page parallel to you at your work surface, with a sheet of scrap paper under the page, and another sheet of scrap paper placed carefully just below the broken edge, exposing approximately half the breadth of the repair paper to be used. The scrap paper on top of the page will mask the page of text—except for the margin to be adhered—while the adhesive is brushed on. Brush adhesive from the center of the scrap paper mask out across the exposed edge; brush, as in the illustration, in a direction opposite you so that adhesive cannot "crawl" under the scrap paper mask. All that is needed is a narrow band of adhesive running along the broken edge of the page—the edge to be hinged into the gutter of the book. After this step, discard the scrap paper and place the page on another piece of clean scrap paper.

2. **Set hinge material into position.**

   Carefully set the Japanese paper hinge strip (cut to size earlier) over the adhesive strip, so that half the breadth of the paper hinge covers the adhered edge and the other half surpasses the broken edge. This becomes the paper hinge. Lower the repair paper with care, seeing that it "lands" straight, and that there is an equal breadth of the paper strip both covering the brushed-on adhesive <u>and</u> overhanging the cut edge of the page. This may be burnished into place by covering with clean scrap paper and either using your hand or the bone folding tool.

3. **Prepare hinged page to be hinged into the book.**

   When the hinged page has dried (in approximately 5 minutes), trim the exposed corners of the hinge with scissors so that the extended portion of the hinge becomes narrower than the portion adhered to the broken page. Trimming avoids the problem of incongruent edges in the gutter area, which would be awkward to remedy. (See Figure 19, which shows the trimmed hinge.)

Figure 19—Hinged page; note how the hinge edges are trimmed at an angle.

Now, with your accomplished masking technique, on a clean sheet of scrap paper set down the hinged page, with the hinge facing up. Place another clean sheet of scrap paper so that *only the overhanging portion* of the Japanese paper hinge shows. Follow through by brushing on adhesive from the scrap paper mask out across the exposed hinge. The line of adhesive resulting will anchor the page into the book. Keep in mind that both adhesion steps are carried out on the same page facing. Discard scrap paper and set the hinge-adhered paper down (face up), so that the book can be positioned for the last steps. "Hurry slowly," as this repair must be accomplished while the adhesive is still wet.

4. Set the hinged page into the gutter.

After confirming the position of the book with that of the page (paying attention to page numbers), hold the book open as much as it comfortably permits. Line up the outer corners of the page to the corners of the other pages in the book, and securely hold down the edge of the page opposite the hinge. With a metal-edged ruler held to the inside margin of the paper hinge (where the exposed adhesive "starts," just at the page break) push carefully and securely into the gutter of the book. Before removing the ruler, carefully slide it in one direction, preventing any adhesion of the hinged page to the ruler itself. (See Figure 21, where the position of the ruler has changed since hinging-in the page in Figure 20.)

Figure 20—Pressing hinged page into place with a metal-edged ruler.

Figure 21—Ruler lifted from book's gutter. (Note position change since Figure 20.)

5. **Finishing the repair.**

Before setting the closed book aside to dry completely (no less than 15 minutes in a dry place), confirm your repair by examining the hinge, wiping off any excess adhesive, and carefully sandwiching the repaired page with waxed paper. Close the book and press under weight until dry.

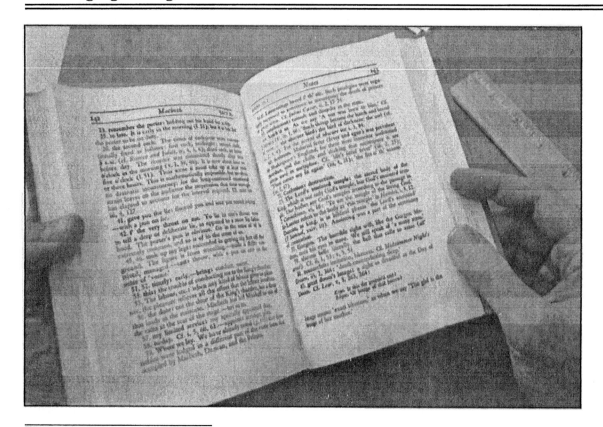

Figure 22—Confirmed repair.

Postscriptum

In the likelihood of even the slightest overhanging of hinged-in pages against the rest of the textblock (particularly along the edge opposite the spine), a finishing trim may be made using a ruler and the Olfa® knife. Place a sheet of cardboard (or a matboard scrap) underneath the hinged page. Make sure the knife has a fresh blade. With the bound-in pages "above" the hinged-in page serving as a guide for placing the ruler, trim carefully along the edge of the ruler. A close trim will help prevent the hinged-in pages from being unnecessarily pulled on as the book is used.

It is suggested that prior to Step 4, when the hinged page is coated with adhesive and set into the gutter, that this careful step be "rehearsed." Some handling problems can be avoided, once acquainted with the procedure that includes the simultaneous holding of an open book with the precise "grafting-in" of a page with a ruler. This procedure may also be successfully done with two sets of hands, one person per function.

6
Case and Textblock Attachment

About Case and Textblock Attachment

This repair becomes necessary when a book's textblock has completely separated from its case (the hard cover). Textblock breaks from cases can be the results of combined deterioration of the super and endpapers, heavy use, or careless handling. Reattaching a textblock to its case is comprised of three processes. The first two specifically treat the textblock: the replacement of the endpaper and the affixing of a new super to the spine. The third part of the process treats the case itself, preparing it to be joined with the repaired textblock. The description in this manual will divide the succession of steps into three phases.

**Required materials for the
complete repair process:**

- Durable pH neutral paper. Paper such as Permalife® is recommended, because it must be acid-free and of strong enough fiber to serve as an endpaper for a bound volume.

- Super. The trade name for the gauze material used for book spines. The super joins the spine to the case via the endpaper (see Figure 11).

- PVA adhesive. For all adhesive needs in this procedure.

- Brush. For the application of PVA adhesive.

- Ruler. For finishing edge-trims.

- Right triangle. For endpaper preparation.

- Olfa® knife. For all paper cutting. Keep a supply of spare blades.

- Bone folding tool. To be used for shaping the endpaper.

- Microspatula. To be used in stripping the old endpaper.

A) Endpaper Replacement

Procedure: Before starting this process, lay aside the case, as it will not be needed until the textblock has been prepared through steps A and B. Begin by examining the textblock itself, checking that the outer pages are tightly attached. The portion of the original endpaper still attached to the textblock may be removed. If there are inscriptions or other valuable information on the original endpapers, these can be hinged to the replacement material. Remove any loose debris from the edges and spine, including any residual pieces of the original super and particles from the broken endpapers.

1. **Preparing new endpapers.**

    Cut two sheets of acid-free paper so that when they are each folded in half, they will moderately exceed the dimension of the book's format. For example, if a book's page measures 6" x 9" (the 9" side being parallel to the spine), a sheet of paper may be cut to 10" x 14", which would fold in half to 7" x 10", overlapping 6" x 9" just enough to be trimmed down specifically to meet the requirements of the book. It is more accurate to trim down than to approximate by a measurement that may not cover enough. When cutting from larger sheets of endpaper material, make note of the direction of the paper's grain. The grain of an endpaper should run parallel to the spine. Grain direction may be determined by wetting a scrap; the wet paper will curl perpendicular to the grain.

Figure 23—Marking exact height of endpaper needed, measuring over the textblock.

2.   Fitting of new endpapers.

After measuring the textblock and cutting 2 sheets of endpaper material, crease both in half (using the bone tool), with the paper grain running parallel to the fold. Next, place the folded endpaper atop the textblock, registering one end precisely along either the top or bottom of the book's textblock (see Figure 23). The left-right dimension is not critical at this stage—as long as it slightly exceeds that of the textblock, it can be trimmed later. With a sharp pencil, mark the point at which one end of the endpaper must be trimmed in order to match the height of the textblock (the dimension parallel to the spine).

With a right triangle registered to the crease in the paper, at a right angle against the pencil mark, carefully cut the excess off with the Olfa® knife.

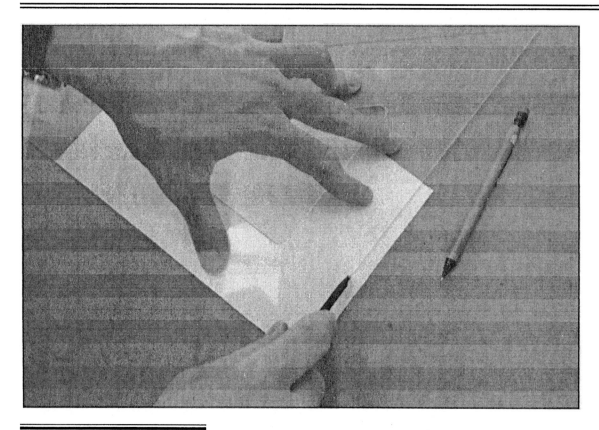

Figure 24—Cutting the endpaper to size, at a right angle.

The endpaper is now ready to be custom fitted to the book. Place the folded end of the endpaper under a ruler parallel to the near edge of your work table, exposing about 1/8" of the creased end of the endpaper. Holding the ruler down tightly, bend up that narrow margin at the creased end, burnishing it with the bone tool against the ruler's edge, producing a bent endpaper joint matching the shoulder of the textblock (see Figure 25).

Figure 25—Bent-edged endpaper and the textblock.

A sharp table edge can also be used successfully. Follow this procedure with both endpapers, making sure that the bend is straight, not having a margin exceeding the curved shoulder of the textblock. Confirm your measurements and the contour of the creased, bent endpapers with the textblock, dry-fitting them. Now the endpapers are ready to be adhered to the textblock.

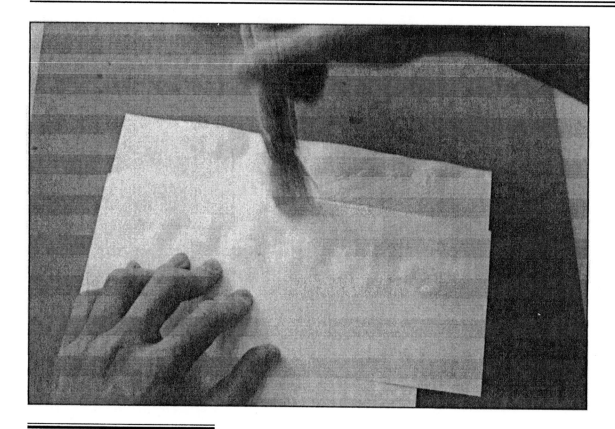

Figure 26—Applying PVA, over scrap-paper mask, to the back of the endpaper's bent margin.

3.   Adhering new endpapers.

On a clean sheet of scrap paper, place the endpaper "face down"; that is, so the bent shoulder margin (along the creased edge of the endpaper) is bending away from you (with an eye at the table-top level, you would see a "triangle" created by the bent endpaper). Next, set down another clean sheet of scrap paper over the endpaper, exposing the bent shoulder only. Masking off the endpaper, except for the bent shoulder (see Figure 26), brush on PVA adhesive, making your brushstrokes emanate from the center of the scrap-paper mask moving out and across the exposed margin of the endpaper. The resultant strip of PVA will anchor the "inside" (facing into the textblock) of an endpaper to the text of the book. Follow through with both endpapers, adhering by masking, then setting into place on both sides of the textblock. Securely work the bent, creased edge of each endpaper into the shoulders of the textblock with your hands. Now, having applied new endpapers, allow at least 5 minutes for the PVA to solidify.

Figure 27—New endpaper adhered to the textblock.

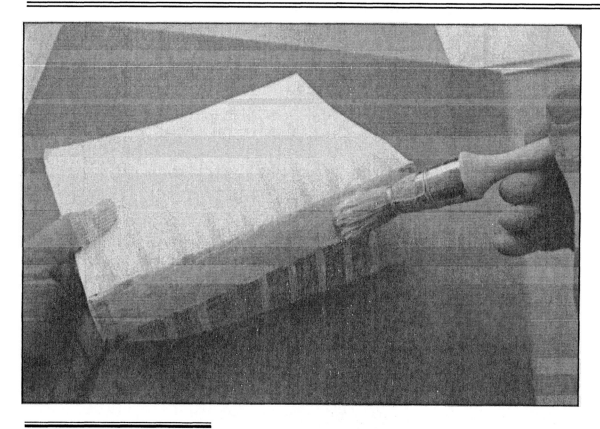

Figure 28—Adhesion of the super to the textblock.

B) Replacement of the Super

Procedure: At this stage, the textblock is ready to have the new super attached. Begin by cutting a piece of super material, with sharp scissors, to dimensions that are approximately ½" shorter than the spine, and leaving approximately 1" to 1½" to the left and right of the spine (see Figure 28). The super will undergird the endpaper, holding the textblock tightly to the case.

After cutting the super to an appropriate size, proceed by brushing PVA directly onto the spine. Afterwards, affix the super so that it is centered on the textblock spine, as it is in Figure 28. When you have secured the placement of the super, conclude the process by brushing another coat of PVA atop the super, assuring a tight seal. The overcoating of PVA may be smoothed out with a finger, also removing excess adhesive. Allow the assembled textblock to dry; the double coat of PVA requires approximately 15 minutes to dry (in a dry environment). Place the textblock down flat on a support (such as a box) letting the super overhang the support while solidifying.

C) Preparing the Case and Attaching the Textblock

Procedure: With the textblock set aside to dry, turn your attention to the case.

1. **Remove material that has been replaced.**
    On a clean work surface, carefully and thoroughly remove the old super and the endpapers, in that order. Remove as much of the old material as possible, especially any loose particles and fibers.

Figure 29—Stripping of the old super from the case.

Figure 30—Prying up the old endpaper using a microspatula.

If endpaper material can be coaxed out of the case by prying up with a microspatula, remove the material, particularly at the corners. Remember that you are preparing a "ground" for affixing the new endpapers and super which are attached to the textblock.

Figure 31—Dry-fitting the textblock to the case.

2. Dry-fit the textblock.

Before examining the fit of textblock and case, trim off the remaining excess endpaper (which overhangs the edge opposite the spine). With the same technique as in hinged-page trimming, set a piece of cardboard under an endpaper and a ruler atop several book pages above the endpaper. Trim endpapers with the Olfa® knife to match the breadth of the text's pages.

With both textblock and case ready to be attached, examine their assembly by fitting them together without adhesive. You can now confirm your measurements and procedures. To dry-fit, place the textblock inside the case, close the case, and reopen the book (one side at a time) checking that the textblock fits comfortably in the case. As Figure 31 shows, the super will lie between the inside of the case and the outermost page of the endpapers. Once the fit is verified, the book is ready to be assembled.

3. Attach textblock to case.

With the textblock and case dry-fit together, set the book down on the work table and carefully open it as in Figure 31. Place a sheet of waxed paper underneath the top endpaper page, and apply PVA adhesive in the following order:

a) under the super (the portion of the super facing the endpaper),

b) above the super (the portion of the super facing into the case),

c) on the top endpaper page (which faces into the case), brush from the center out to the edges (the waxed paper sheet should catch any excess PVA).

Close the book, and follow the same order for the other side of the book.

Use care not to allow adhesive to affect the spine. It is not necessary to coat the case with adhesive; "activating" the endpapers is sufficient.

Complete the assembly by closing the book, and burnishing the exterior of the case. Carefully open the book to check for any problems such as wrinkling of endpapers or unevenness of textblock placement—especially while the glue is still wet. Leave the waxed paper in, as the interleaving will continue to catch excess PVA under the pressure of burnishing. As with the hinge-tightening procedure, set a skewer into the exterior joints (both front and back covers), and burnish with the bone tool. After burnishing, the waxed paper interleaving should be replaced by clean pieces to prevent any off-set adhesive from affecting either the case exterior or other pages. Place the closed book under weight and allow to dry overnight to allow the PVA some "curing" time.

Figure 32—Completed repair; the textblock is reattached to the case.

Postscriptum

As lengthy as this process may appear, with phases for the textblock and for the case, the repair can be completed (up to the final drying stage) in less than 30 minutes. Work methodically and with batches of books, keeping careful track of their respective components, so that something is always being assembled, minimizing "down time." Your workspace should be organized and very well lit. The joining of materials is precise work, but thankfully water-soluble adhesives are reversible. Some fascinating varieties of endpapers are available (some "marbled" by hand) and if these seem interesting to you, give priority to the necessary properties of neutral pH content and durability, as well as cost. Permalife®, which meets the requirements for endpapers, can be purchased in a cream color, making for an all-purpose "neutral" endpaper for library collections.

7
Cloth Rebacking

About Cloth Rebacking

The rebacking of a book refers to the replacement of the textblock spine support material, including encasing a new spine with new book cloth. As the terms imply, this is a repair process specific to cloth case-bound books. This process also implies that a book's cloth case is in sufficiently good condition to justify a basic rebacking, as opposed to a complete re-binding to be done at a bindery. Generally speaking, when a spine backing has significantly outworn the rest of the case, it is due to repeated pulling on the headcap area (the top of the spine) when removing a book from the shelf. This tends to occur with greater frequency in research libraries, where books that are heavily used are kept in collections for longer periods of time. Rebacking also tends to be necessary among reference books, which are frequently used—often in haste—and usually support heavy textblocks. The repair process is uncomplicated, and with the exception of the spine and cloth materials, makes use of tools you will already have on hand for the other processes.

Figure 33—Tools needed for cloth rebacking: book cloth and Bristol board at left, Olfa® knife, microspatula, bone folding tool, and ruler in center—with PVA and brush at right.

Required Materials:

- Book cloth. This is available in various colors and sold as sheets (to be cut to specific sizes) or on rolls for rebacking use.

- Bristol board. This is a type of card stock, available at art supply stores. Make sure it is acid-free. Bristol board is sold in various weights (thicknesses); 10-point, or "2-ply" is suggested for this purpose.

- PVA adhesive. To be used for encasing the spine and for attaching the new backing to the case.

- Brush. Must be free of contaminating residues, for application of PVA.

- Olfa® knife. For cutting Bristol board and cloth. Keep spare blades available.

- Scrap paper. Keep plenty of clean scrap paper on hand for steps involving the application of adhesive.

- Ruler and right triangle. As measuring and cutting edges. The right triangle is necessary for preparing the Bristol board spine.

- Bone folding tool. For burnishing and creasing applications.

- Microspatula. For prying up cloth attached to cases without causing damage.

- Sharp pencil. For use in preparing the spine.

- Cutting surface. Either a thick sheet of cardboard or a "self-healing" plastic cutting base.

Procedure: The process of cloth rebacking begins with the removal of a broken spine (if it is still attached), followed by the forming of a new spine, encasing the new spine in book cloth, then attaching this new backing to the book. This method has the new backing set into the cloth case, rather than overlapping it, preventing any aggravation of the backing during handling and reshelving.

1. **Remove the broken spine**.

    If the book's spine is still loosely attached (as the example in Figure 34), carefully remove it by running a light cut along the attached joint with the Olfa® knife. Prevent damage to the textblock spine by using a light touch, which also preserves any information on the original spine. Tearing at the superficially-attached spine may also contort the fibers of the intact case. Set aside the original spine.

Figure 34—Cutting a strip of cloth on the board, along the shoulder joint.

2. **Prepare boards for new backing.**

The next steps concern preparing the case itself to have the new backing inserted. With the original spine removed, use a ruler and your Olfa® knife, and in one light linear pass, cut a margin of cloth along the length of the spine (see Figure 34). A margin of approximately ¼" (or 1 cm.) is recommended. Before removing the cut strip of cloth, make some careful side cuts (in a "letter-opener" fashion) at the top and bottom of the case boards, beginning from the shoulders (see Figure 35).

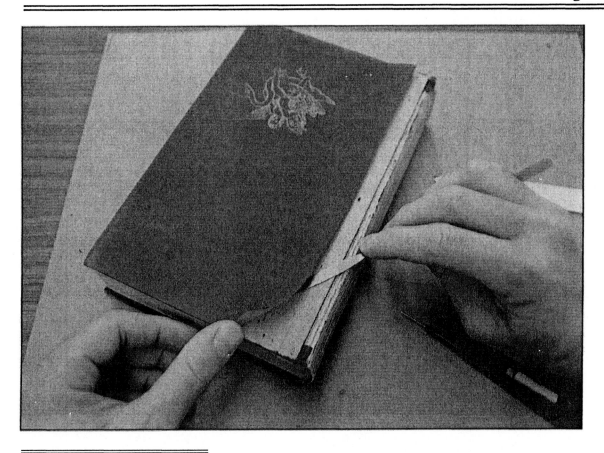

Figure 35—Prying up cloth with a microspatula. Note side cut near my thumb.

These delicate side cuts just made, exceeding the margin of the cut strip of cloth (by not more than an inch) will allow for a smooth attachment of the new backing. Before setting the book aside, carefully pry up the cloth with the microspatula, along the cut only, as the original cloth pulled up along with the new backing will require adhesive (see Figure 35).

3.   Measure and cut the new spine.

Now we shall focus on constructing a new backing which will be custom-fitted to the book, beginning with the spine. With a strip of Bristol board exceeding the dimension required for the new spine, measure for the width of the spine by bending the strip against the back of the textblock (see Figure 36).

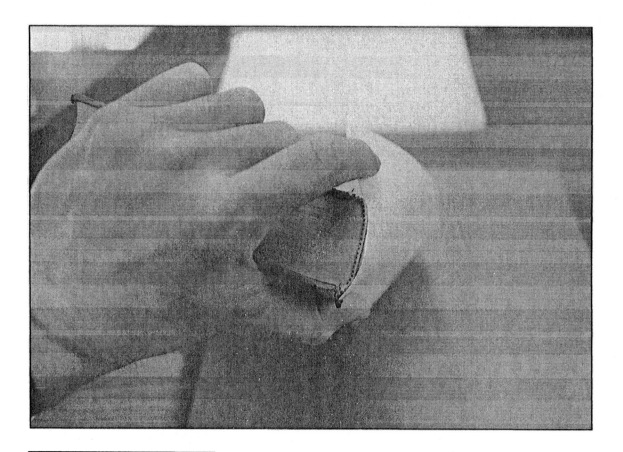

Figure 36—Measurement of Bristol board to book.

By measuring in this way, the new spine will meet the specific dimensions of the original case. When measuring, be sure to cover the area of the spine and *not* that of the shoulder joints. The Bristol board is flexible enough to be held in place, once a width is ascertained. With a pencil, scribe exactly where the new spine's width should be cut. Setting the book aside, cut the indicated width of the Bristol board using a right triangle, making sure the cut width is square to the length of the strip. Now set the Bristol board strip, cut to match the width of the thickness of the textblock, down on your work surface and physically measure it against the *boards* of the case. It is critical that the measurement of the width of the spine be made against the width of the textblock, and the measurement of the length of the textblock be made against the boards of the case. With the new spine cut to specification, slice not more than 1/8" (3 mm.) off the length (which runs along the shoulder of the book). Cutting an ever-so-slightly shorter spine (than the length of the boards) will even out as the bulk of the folded book cloth compensates for the cut. Double-check that the new spine is the correct size.

Figure 37—Trimming the length of the new spine.

4. **Attach cloth to the new spine**.

Book cloth is manufactured with a shiny side, which is generally intended to face in, and a dull side that generally faces out for presentation. Either side of the cloth may be used for facing out. The dull side, however, is less susceptible to scratches and scuff marks made with use. Begin by coating a scrap piece of paper, which is larger than the spine's dimensions, with PVA adhesive. Next, place the Bristol board cut spine on the coating of adhesive, carefully lift it off with the microspatula and set it down on an oversized piece of book cloth. The cloth will eventually wrap around the Bristol board spine, so leave a generous margin of cloth for a starting periphery. Also bear in mind that you are placing the new spine piece atop the facing of cloth which will face *in* towards the book spine, not out for presentation.

Figure 38—Bristol board spine adhered to the shiny side of the book cloth.

With the Bristol board spine piece adhered to the inside of the backing cloth, burnish tightly with the bone folder. Trim carefully around the adhered bristol spine with knife and ruler. The thickness of my ruler (see Figure 39) provided a sufficient breadth of cloth margin. With the cloth backing trimmed around the spine piece, make cuts with a pair of scissors above and below the spine piece (see Figure 39).

Figure 39—Cuts in spine cloth to be folded over.

The two cuts, as seen in Figure 39, are to reach the spine piece, and be centered above and below the long side of the spine. The purpose of the cuts is to provide for a smooth curvature when accommodating the contour of the book during assembly.

Figure 40—The fold of the cut cloth over the spine should be very slightly angled.

The next step leads to the completion of the cloth-backed spine. Note in Figure 40 how the cut just made above and below the Bristol board spine piece enables the cloth to be folded precisely over, at an extremely slight angle. Note how the folded over "flaps" created by the cut are to be folded over (and adhered) angled *in* towards the center. The angle should be slight enough to allow for that needed curvature, and enough to notice an overlap of the folded-over corners (at the center). Try this first without adhesive, then, over a clean piece of scrap paper, brush PVA only on the cloth to be folded, fold over, crease, and burnish down.

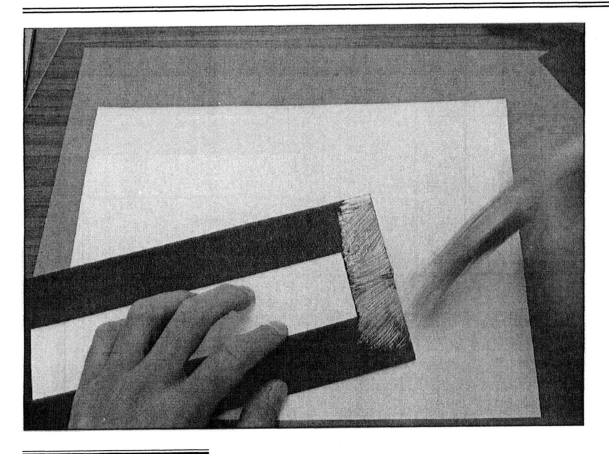

Figure 41—Brushing PVA onto cloth. Note that adhesive is applied only to the ends.

Remember that a minimal amount of PVA will effectively adhere the cloth. Excess adhesive will seep out from the adhered area during burnishing. It is suggested that when working with these cloth processes, your brush is not dripping with PVA, but is somewhat dry for application. Figure 42 shows how the new cloth-backed spine appears after burnishing and prior to shaping for adhesion to the book's case.

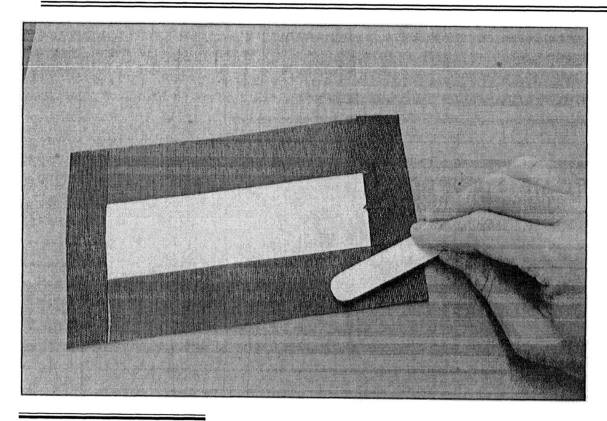

Figure 42—Prepared spine, ready to be shaped.

Figure 43—Curved backing with book.

5. Fit the new backing to the book.

So that the new backing can be fitted, it must be shaped to fit the book and confirmed by dry-fitting. Use the edge of a table and carefully turn the inside of the spine piece against the edge. The idea is not to form the new backing into a narrow tube, or crease it, but to curve it to match the type of book being repaired.

Figure 43 shows the curved backing ready to be dry-fit with the book. Dry-fit by carefully tucking the new cloth of the backing under the original cloth of the case. Make sure that the new spine is directly behind the textblock super. Stand the book up to further check that the new backing fits. Especially confirm the length of the new spine, that the sliver cut from the Bristol board has now been compensated for by the top and bottom folds of cloth. With an affirmative dry-fit, the backing need not be detached for adhesion, but simply held carefully in place.

Figure 44—Dry-fitting the new backing to the book.

6. **Adhere new backing and complete the process**.

With a confirmed dry-fit, and with the new backing in place, score the shoulder joints with the edge of the bone folder, running the length of the outer ridge. Scoring the shoulder joints helps to form the backing around the book's contour.

Figure 45—Brushing adhesive onto the inside of the cloth backing.

To adhere, treating one side of the book at a time, brush PVA adhesive along the inside portion of the cloth that will be tucked into the board's cloth. Work over a sheet of scrap paper, making sure that no adhesive affects the spine or the cloth directly above and below the spine (see Figure 45). Adhere the new cloth to the board exposed by the cuts made at the first step of this process. Burnish, then brush PVA on the inside portion of the original case cloth. Use a minimal amount of adhesive, but enough for the cloths to bond and not leave upturned corners. Burnish tightly into place, burnish the shoulder joint, then repeat the process for the other side of the book.

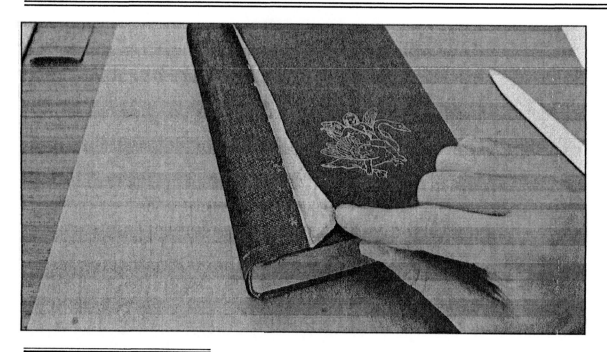

Figure 46—Adhesion of the old cloth over the new, which is tucked in.

When adhering the second side of the book (having first anchored one side to the case), hold the backing firmly over the spine area of the book, almost to the point of stretching the backing, to assure a snug fit. Do not create an excess of slack cloth over the super. Burnish the adhered areas with the flat side of the bone folder, and the shoulder joints with the short edge. As a final touch-up, dab a fairly dry brush of PVA to the top and bottom case edges where the original cloth was sliced; work the cloth together by pinching with two fingers (see Figure 47). A sufficient drying time is approximately 8 hours in a dry place.

Figure 47—Attached cloth backing. The new cloth is tucked underneath the original board cloth.

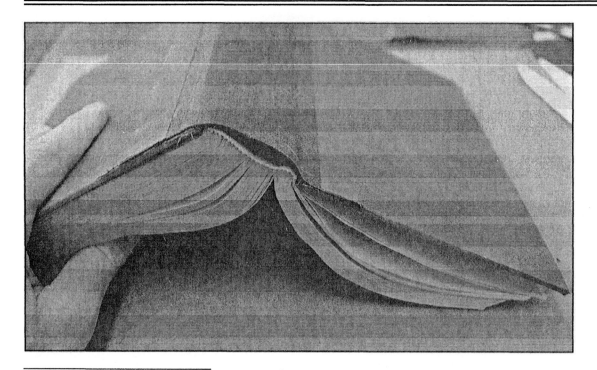

Figure 48—New backing seen from the edge. Note the degree of flexibility in the backing.

Postscriptum

When considering whether rebacking is the appropriate measure for a book in disrepair, make sure that the case (apart from the spine) is in good enough condition. Boards may be damaged to the extent that a complete re-binding may be necessary. In performing this repair, remember the precise aspects of cutting the Bristol board spine piece. Be sure that it is as wide as the back of the textblock (less the shoulders) and as long as the boards are long, less not more than ⅛" (just a couple of millimeters). Finally, when adhering the new backing, make sure it is tight to the back of the textblock; there will still be sufficient flexibility for the book to open and close (see Figure 48). No adhesive should interfere with the spine, or hold the spine to the super (as is customary with paperback books), and adhesive should not be brushed on the boards themselves.

8
Retitling

About Retitling

Retitling becomes necessary when a book has been rebacked. The original spine has been removed, which included the title and call number. Also, the spine may have been decorative. With these considerations in mind, the original spine may be worth preserving. Another option is to create a new identifying spine title, and affixing this to the rebacked book.

Required Materials:

- Spine material, either the original or a replacement paper title label.

- PVA adhesive for attaching the titles to the spine.

- Brush to apply PVA adhesive.

- Right triangle for squaring edges and to use as a cutting straight edge.

- Olfa® knife for cutting spine titles.

- Scrap paper to be used for the coating of adhesive.

- Bone folding tool for burnishing the attached title piece.

Procedure: As stated, either a replacement title label can be made for attachment to the new backing, or the original spine may be attached. If the original spine label is preferred, simply peel away the cloth label from the old cardboard backing material (the old spine was sliced away in the first step of the rebacking process). Carefully pull away any excess paper particles and fibers.

Figure 49—Trimming off the old spine, and squaring the edges.

1. **Trim original spine label**.

   If one is going to re-use the original spine label, remove its cardboard backing, peeling away excess material, and place the label face up on your cutting surface. With the Olfa® knife, a triangle, and a ruler, trim the label so that it has crisp right angles. Make sure the knife blade is sharp, so that the knife does not pull fibers away from the label as it drags across the old cloth material.

2. Apply adhesive.

The next step is to coat a scrap piece of paper (exceeding the size of the spine label) with PVA. Set the label, face up, on the coating of adhesive; press down and carefully pry up with the microspatula.

Figure 50—Original label adhered to the new spine.

3. Affix label to spine.

With the book's spine facing up, gently set the title label down on the spine. Before pressing the label into place, the wet PVA having some workability, form the label into place. Burnish firmly, either directly with the bone folder or with a piece of scrap paper between the folding tool and the spine label.

Postscriptum

With this process, we can employ some creativity concerning the maintenance of title information, using original identifying material or replacing the old spine label with a new one. If the information on a damaged original is preferred, fragments of the spine label may be affixed to the rebacked book. Replacement labels may be computer-generated, making them clear and easily read on the shelves, and may include library barcodes. Labels which are narrower and shorter than the spine (see Figure 50) are far less likely to peel off the book than if the label exactly meets the dimensions of the spine backing.

Post Postscriptum

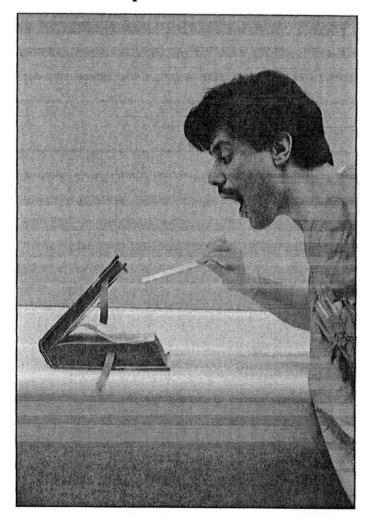

A strengthened *Strong's Concordance* affirms an "ahhh" for the author.

Appendix 1

Wheat-Starch
Paste Recipe

1. Place one cup of wheat starch and five or six cups of distilled water in the top of a very clean double boiler.

2. Mix well and let stand at least 20 minutes.

3. Fill the bottom part of double boiler with a small amount of cold water so that the upper section does not touch the water.

4. Place on medium high heat and cook, stirring constantly with a clean wire whisk.

5. When the paste begins to thicken (this may happen right away), reduce heat and continue stirring.

6. Stir for about half an hour; then remove from the stove. The paste should be thick and translucent. As it cooks and thickens, it will become more difficult to stir. To aid in stirring, a wooden spoon may be substituted for the wire whisk, but the spoon should be one that has not been used for the preparation of food.

7. When cooked, the paste should be transferred to a clean container for storage. It should be allowed to cool before use. Prior to use, the paste should be strained. A Japanese paste strainer works well for this.

[Author's note: To prepare a smaller quantity, the mixing ratio of 1 part wheat starch to 5 parts water may also be applied with tablespoon measurements. Prepared wheat-starch paste lasts approximately four days.]

Sherelyn Ogden, ed., "Repairing Paper Artifacts," in *Preservation of Library and Archival Materials: A Manual* (Andover, Mass.: Northeast Document Conservation Center, 1994), p. 2. Used with permission.

Appendix 2
Supply Retailers

Bookmakers
6601 66th Avenue, Suite 101
Riverdale, MD 20737
(301) 459-3384
FAX (301) 459-7629
   [Supplies, tools and equipment for book and paper conservation, and hand bookbinding.]

Conservation Resources International
8000-H Forbes Place
Springfield, VA 22151
(800) 634-6932
FAX (703) 321-0629
   [Strong selection of conservation tools, materials, enclosures; thorough catalogue.]

Gaylord Bros.
P.O. Box 4901
Syracuse, NY 13221-4901
(800) 634-6307 (customer service & assistance)
(800) 448-6160 (ordering)
Website: http://www.gaylord.com/
   [Strong on conservation supplies—adhesives, heat-set tissue, Reemay®, etc.]

TALAS
568 Broadway, Suite 107
New York, NY 10012
(212) 736-7744
FAX: (212) 465-8722
    [Conservation supplies, including adhesives, paste strainers]

University Products
517 Main Street
P.O. Box 101
Holyoke, MA 01041-0101
(800) 762-1165
FAX (800) 532-9281
Website: http://www.universityproducts.com
    [Conservation tools, equipment, papers, and display materials]

Appendix 3

Glossary of Selected Terms

BACKING

The process of forming a reinforcing covering for the spine of a textblock, producing ridges, or shoulders, and connecting the boards of a case-bound book.

BOARDS

Thick papers or chipboard used to support the sides and produce the case of a bound book.

BOOK CLOTH

Flexible material, from woven fabric to polymer-coated cloth, such as buckram, used for covering books.

BRISTOL BOARD

A fine card stock, manufactured in a variety of sizes and thicknesses. Acid-free, cotton-fiber Bristol board is available.

BURNISH

To smoothen or crease by friction. For book and paper applications, bone folding tools are popular burnishers.

CASE

A book cover, comprising the covering material (such as book cloth), the boards, and the spine-backing inlay.

CASE-BINDING
: The preparation of the case (the cover) prior to its attachment to the textblock.

ENDPAPER
: The leaves of paper fitted to the front and end pages of a book, and adhered to the insides of the boards and the shoulders of the textblock.

GUTTER
: Adjoining inner margins in a pair of facing pages in a book.

HINGE
: Inside channels along which the endpapers are adhered to the textblock of a book.

JOINT (or, EXTERIOR JOINT)
: The grooves on either side of a book, adjacent to the spine.

pH VALUE (also known as hydrogen-ion concentration)
: Verification of pH (potential of hydrogen) is critical when selecting materials for permanence, as a low pH rating (below 7) indicates acid content. A neutral pH of 7 is both alkaline and stable.

POLYVINYL ACETATE
: A strong vinyl resin adhesive which is water based and does not contain flammable solvents.

SPINE
: Term used to describe the bound end of a textblock and its outer covering material. The outer spine, or backing, usually bears identifying bibliographic information.

SUPER
: Also referred to as mull, is a coarse cotton mesh material, adhered to the spine of a textblock.

TEXTBLOCK
: The signatures or leaves (configuration of pages) comprising the body of a book, not including the endpapers or case.

Appendix 4
For Further Reading

Baird, Brian J. "The Goals and Objectives of Collections Conservation." *Restaurateur* 13 (4) 1992: 149–161.
   [Efficient collections conservation, coordinated and accomplished within a library, upholds the institution's mission to preserve and provide access to the materials. In-house repair programs, as well as staff and user education, is emphasized.]

Bevacqua, Joanna, and Rafat Ispahany. "Book Repair in the Community College Library." *Conservation Administration News* 46 (July 1991): 8–11.
   [Describes the establishing of a library book repair unit, with clear directives and a thorough bibliography.]

Clapp, Anne F. *Curatorial Care of Works of Art on Paper.* New York: N. Lyons, 1987.
   [Covers environmental aspects and effects on paper-based materials. Chapter themes include dry cleaning, mending edge-tears, and formulas for adhesives and alkaline solutions for aqueous treatment.]

Glaister, Geoffrey Ashall. *Encyclopedia of the Book*, 2nd ed. Newcastle, DE: Oak Knoll, 1996.
   [Dictionary comprising the craft of book production, the history of books, printing, and typography; and prominent individuals involved in these fields. Illustrated with photographs and drawings.]

Greenfield, Jane. *Books: Their Care and Repair.* New York: H. W. Wilson, 1983.
   [Thorough repair manual, embellished with effective line drawings. Hinge and joint repairs are included among book and paper treatments. In addition, there are chapters describing pamphlet binding and exhibition techniques.]

MacDonald, Eric. "Creating a Preservation Department from Existing Staff Resources." *Conservation Administration News* 55 (October 1993): 6.
    [A successful interdepartmental coordinated effort to set up and maintain a library book preservation department.]

Morrow, Carolyn Clark, and Carole Dyal. *Conservation Treatment Procedures: A Manual of Step-by-Step Procedures for the Maintenance and Repair of Library Materials*, 2nd ed. Littleton, CO: Libraries Unlimited, 1986.
    [A well-illustrated manual including book repair procedures, phase-box production, and organizing a conservation workshop.]

Roberts, Matt, and Don Etherington. *Bookbinding and the Conservation of Books: A Dictionary of Descriptive Terminology.* Washington, DC: Library of Congress, 1982.
    [Dictionary focusing on bookbinding and book conservation, covering technical and chemical terms and pertinent physical materials.]

Ritzenthaler, Mary Lynn. *Preserving Archives and Manuscripts.* Chicago: Society of American Archivists, 1993.
    [Coverage of preservation issues incorporates administrative aspects as well as specific treatments for paper materials and a chapter on setting up a work space.]

"SAA Basic Archival Conservation Program: Conservation Techniques." *Society of American Archivists Newsletter* (May 1982).
    [Techniques for surface-cleaning, paper-mending, and fastener-removal are described.]

"SAA Basic Archival Conservation Program: Implementing a Conservation Program." *Society of American Archivists Newsletter* (September 1982).
    [Specifies environmental requirements for paper-based collections, integrating preservation into a repository's program, and setting up an in-house treatment area.]

Reader's Notes

Chapter 1

Reader's Notes
(continued)

Chapter 2

Reader's Notes
(continued)

Chapter 3

Reader's Notes
(continued)

Chapter 4

Reader's Notes
(continued)

Chapter 5

Reader's Notes
(continued)

Chapter 6

Reader's Notes
(continued)

Chapter 7

Reader's Notes
(continued)

Chapter 8

Reader's Notes
(continued)

Index